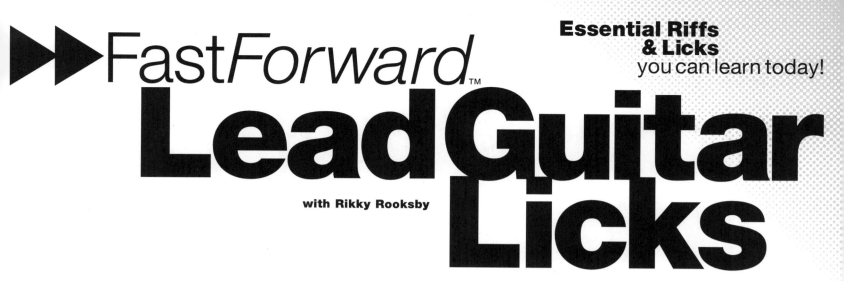

▶▶ *FastForward*™

Lead Guitar Licks

Essential Riffs & Licks you can learn today!

with Rikky Rooksby

T0058838

Wise Publications
London / New York / Sydney / Paris / Copenhagen / Madrid

Exclusive Distributors:
Music Sales Limited
14-15 Berners Street, London W1T 3LJ, UK.
Music Sales Pty Limited
20 Resolution Drive, Caringbah, NSW 2229, Australia.
Music Sales Corporation
257 Park Avenue South, New York, NY10010,
United States of America.

Order No. AM92448
ISBN 0-7119-4524-1
This book © Copyright 1997 by Wise Publications.

Book design by Michael Bell Design.
Edited and arranged by Rikky Rooksby.
Music processed by Seton Music Graphics.
Cover photography by George Taylor.
Cover instrument kindly loaned by
Rhodes Music Company Limited.
Text photographs courtesy of Adrian Boot,
Harry Goodwin and London Features International.
Printed and bound in the United Kingdom.

Your Guarantee of Quality:
As publishers, we strive to produce every book to
the highest commercial standards.
The music has been freshly engraved and the book has
been carefully designed to minimise awkward page turns
and to make playing from it a real pleasure.
Particular care has been given to specifying acid-free,
neutral-sized paper made from pulps which have not
been elemental chlorine bleached.
This pulp is from farmed sustainable forests and
was produced with special regard for the environment.
Throughout, the printing and binding have
been planned to ensure a sturdy, attractive publication
which should give years of enjoyment.
If your copy fails to meet our high standards, please
inform us and we will gladly replace it.

www.musicsales.com

Introduction 4

Start It Up
The Minor Pentatonic Scale 5
The Pull-Off 8
The Hammer-On And Slide 9

Through The Bends
String-Bending 11
The Golden Rules For String-Bending 11
Vibrato 13

First Mile 17

Out Of Town 19

Changing Gear
Playing In The Open Position 21

Stepping Free
Part 1 24
Part 2 25

Pedal To The Floor
Playing Above The 12th Fret 27

Horizon 31

One Particular Place To Go
Chuck Berry Style Licks 32

Hubcap Lipstick 39

Travelling In Style
The Major Pentatonic Scale 40

One For The Road 45

Oh Chevrolet!
An Extended Solo 47
Section 1 47
Section 2 51
Section 3 54
Oh Chevrolet! 56

Guide To Guitar 61

Introduction

Hello, and welcome to ▶▶**Fast***Forward* Congratulations on purchasing a product that will improve your playing and provide you with hours of pleasure. All the music in this book has been specially created by professional musicians to give you maximum value and enjoyability.

If you already know how to 'drive' your instrument but you'd like to do a little customising, you've pulled in at the right place. We'll put you on the fast track to playing the kinds of riffs and patterns that today's professionals rely on.

We'll provide you with a vocabulary of riffs that you can apply in a wide variety of musical situations, with a special emphasis on giving you the techniques that will help you in a band situation. That's why every music example in this book comes with a full-band audio track so that you get your chance to join in.

All players and all bands get their sounds and styles by drawing on the same basic building blocks. With ▶▶**Fast***Forward* you'll quickly learn these, and then be ready to use them to create your own style.

Lead Guitar Licks

If you take Chuck Berry's 'Johnny B. Goode' or Scotty Moore on Elvis's 'Hound Dog' as a rough starting point, rock lead guitar has been around for nearly 40 years. In that time the basic design of rock guitar has gone from a few simple blueprints to a vast number of styles. Just like a motor company with lots of different models, there are many rock lead styles. Some are fast, some are slow; some are flashy, some just cruise. Steve Vai, Johnny Marr, The Edge, James Hetfield, Jimmy Page, Eddie Van Halen, Jeff Beck and Carlos Santana are all rock players but their styles are highly individual.

In this book you will find some road-tested ideas. They've been around quite a time, but players are still giving them a re-spray and taking them out for a spin. Remember that much of the lead guitar you have heard will have been fast, rhythmically complicated and full of difficult ornamentation such as string-bending.

The ideas in this book are kept simple and played at slow to medium tempo.

Each example is given in musical score and in guitar tablature. With the latter each number indicates the fret at which the note is played, each line is a string. If you find it hard to remember which way up they go, think always of pitch: high notes are above low notes, therefore the high-sounding string (1st E) is at the top. Underneath the TAB you will find suggested left-hand fingerings (index = 1, middle = 2, ring = 3, little = 4). Other TAB symbols will be explained as we go along.

Each musical example is played once with the lead guitar, and once without. The first is for you to learn by listening, the second 'play-along' track is for you to practise.

The examples have a one-bar count-in.

Start It Up
The Minor Pentatonic Scale

Music is like an engine with four parts: melody, harmony, rhythm and 'spirit'. By 'spirit' we mean the expression of feeling, music as a way of communicating from the heart.

Melody is a curve of notes you find yourself whistling or singing. Harmony is the chords that make up the music. Rhythm is the beat. Good lead playing is no exception. It should have all four firing.

A good lead break will have rhythm, it will have harmony in that it will fit with the chords underneath, it will have melody, and it should convey real feeling.

Our backing musicians are going to provide four and eight bar phrases in the key of A major.

To start with they're just going to give us an A chord to play over. So what notes do we play?

Our first resource might be the scale of A major: A B C♯ D E F♯ G♯. But this won't give us the typical 'tough' rock lead sound.

We need to move on in the showroom and go for something more basic – with performance rather than comfort.

We need a scale that won't be too sensitive to our mistakes. Following the tuning notes on the audio, here's the scale:

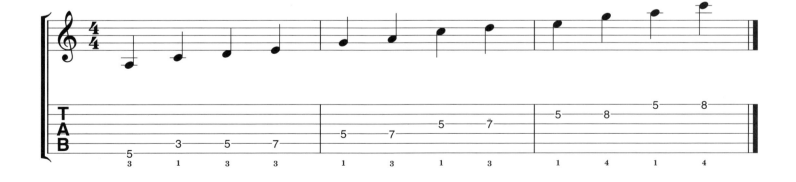

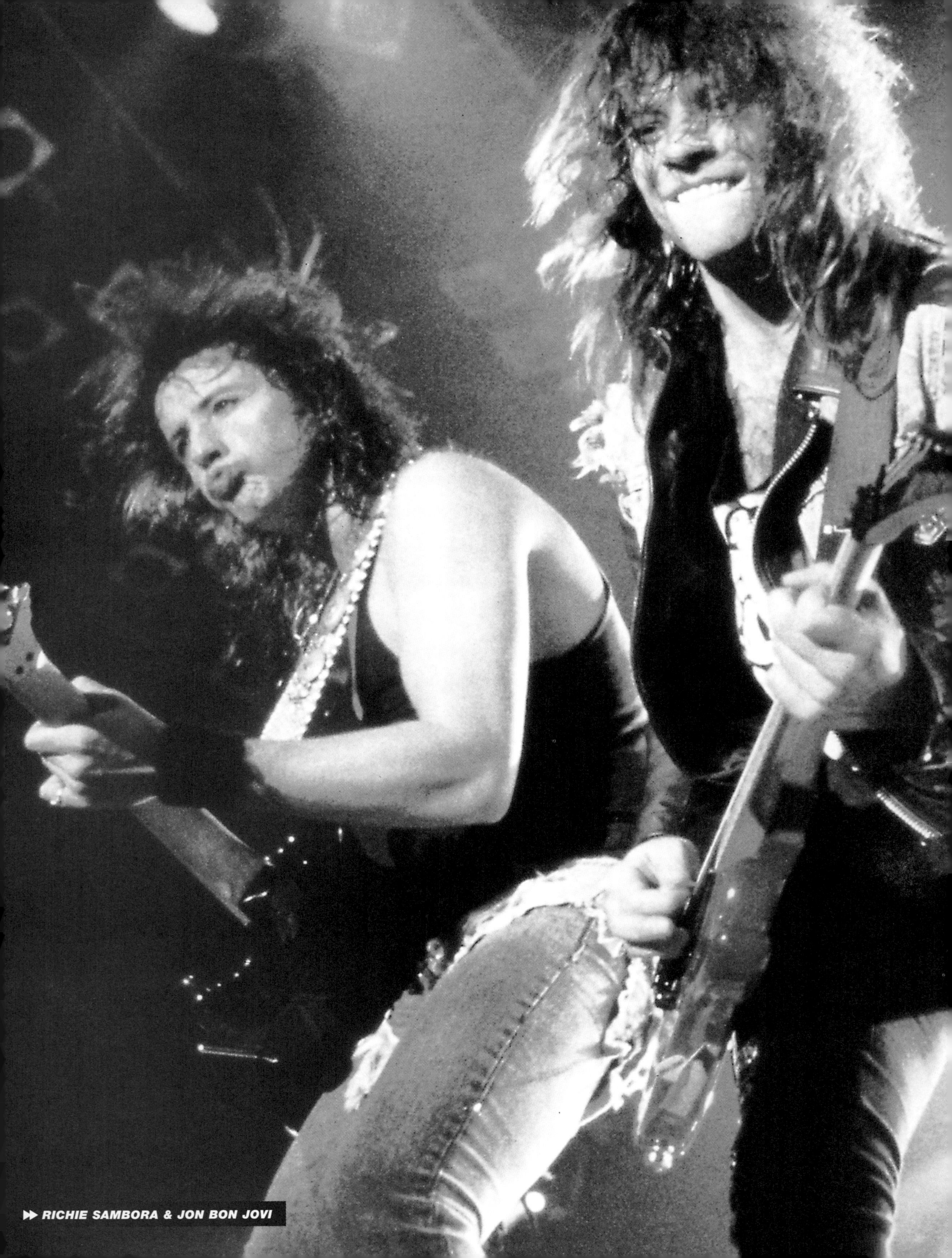

▶▶ RICHIE SAMBORA & JON BON JOVI

This scale is called A pentatonic minor. Pentatonic means 5 notes, such as A C D E G. Normally you wouldn't play a minor scale in a major key, but in rock / blues the 'clash' of notes helps to define the music's particular sound.

Play the scale steadily and slowly using alternate down-and-up strokes of your pick.

Before doing any guitar playing it's a good idea to warm your fingers up with a few scales.

Example 3+4 extends the scale and enables you to go a little further up the neck.

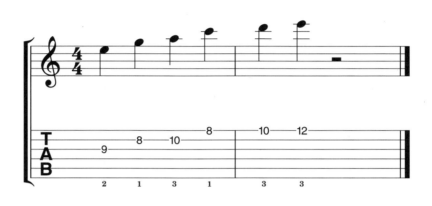

A scale is only potential, like an engine idling. We have to engage melody-harmony-rhythm-spirit to make music. We take some of these notes and shape them, like this:

TRACKS 5+6

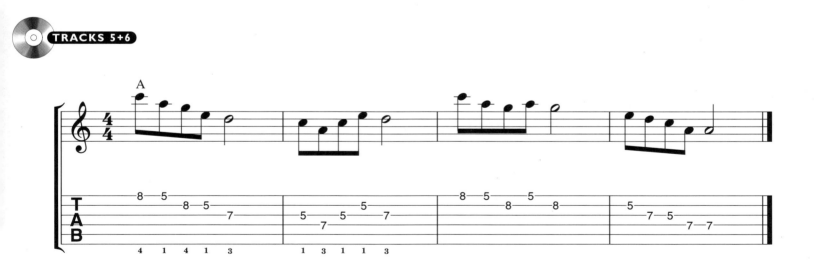

We've got melody, the notes fit with the harmony of the backing, and we have a repeated rhythm. But something's missing. We're lacking expression.

These notes sound like they're not going anywhere. This is where we bring in some extra power.

The Pull-Off

Let's play the last example again, with
some pull-offs (**P**). You'll see these marked in
Example 7+8 as a curved line linking two
descending notes.

In bar 1 put your first and third fingers down
before you start. Play the first note then pull your
3rd finger down and off the string. This will
produce the note at the 5th fret. Then do the
same thing on the 2nd string.

You need to keep your 1st finger fixed in place
each time.

TRACKS 7+8

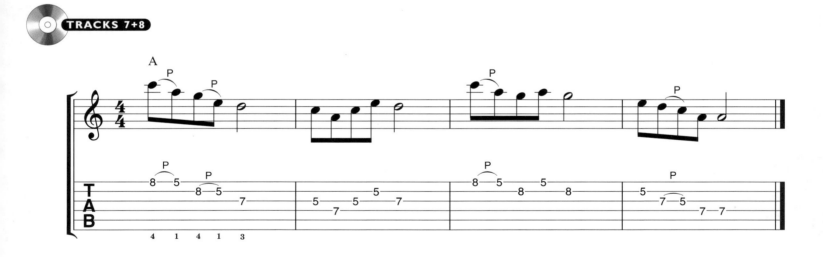

The Hammer-On And Slide

If you reverse this action you get a hammer-on (H). In the next example, after hitting the G at the 5th fret, you hammer your 3rd finger onto the 7th fret to get the next note.

You can also change the feel of notes by sliding to them. The very last note is approached by a very quick slide with the 3rd finger. Keep the finger pressed against the fretboard.

TRACKS 9+10

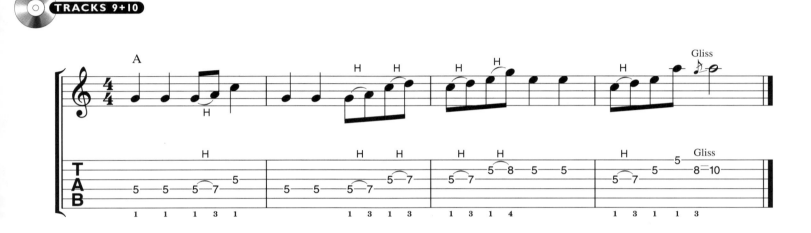

Remember, with these three techniques only the first note is picked, the second is created by the left hand. Next we can combine hammer-ons and pull-offs. In bar 2 of Example 11+12, two

of the same notes on the stave are joined by a curved line. This is called a tie. It means that the note lasts for the duration of both but only the first is struck.

TRACKS 11+12

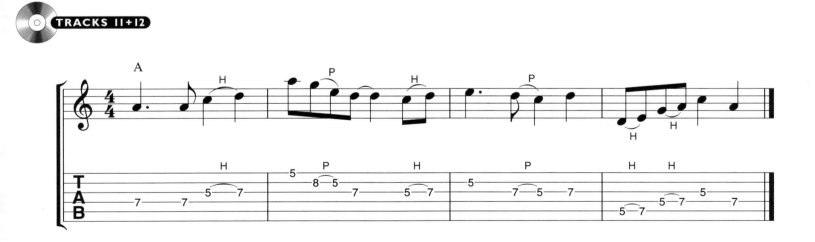

So far, so good. But there's one more technique which is essential to rock lead. With this, we'll be motoring. It's the bend.

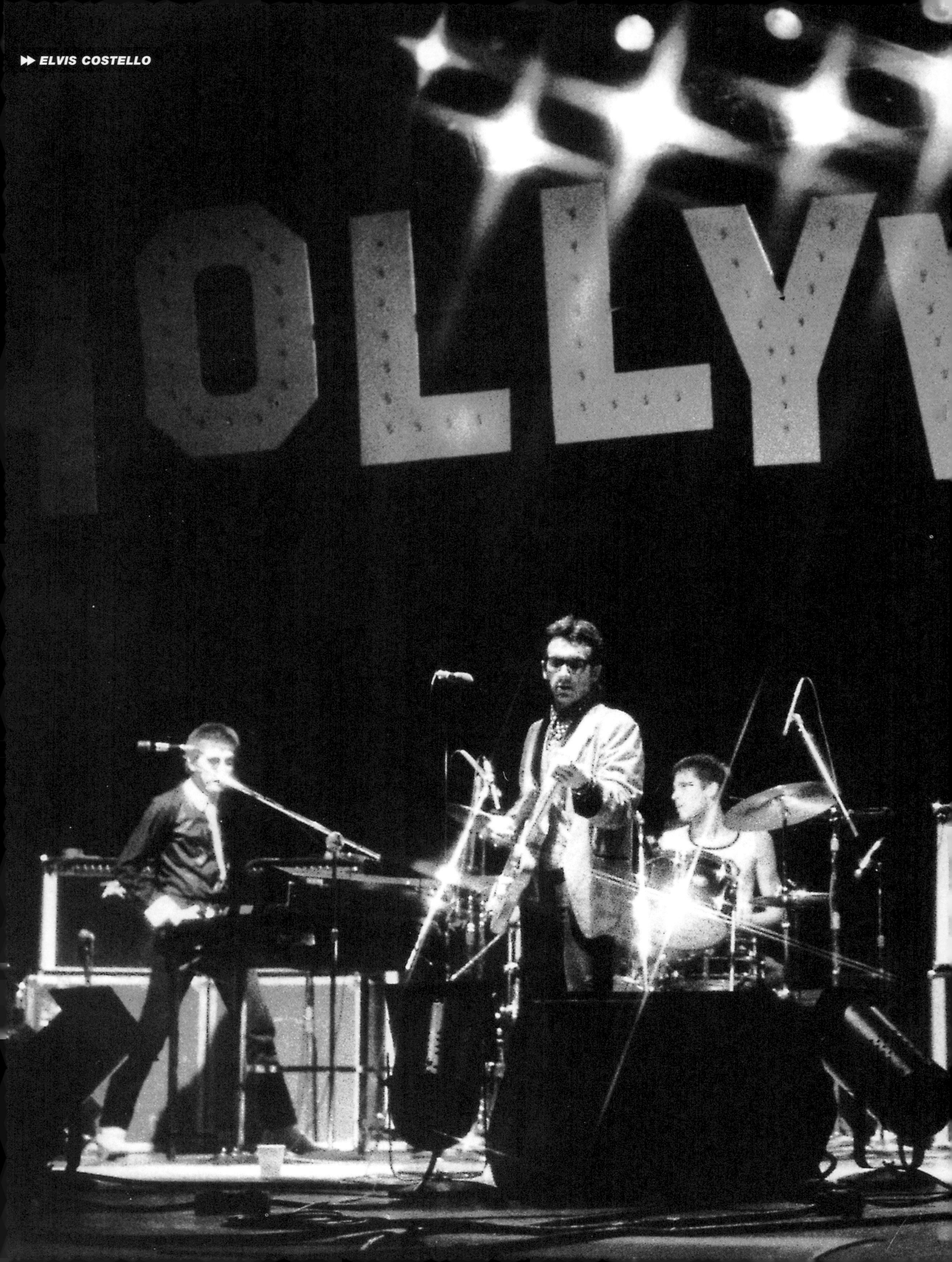
OLLY

Through The Bends
String-Bending

The unforgettable wail and cry of the electric guitar is a combination of string-bending with amplification and distortion. On the guitar not only does the same note occur in more than one place, you can bend up to it from another note.

This creates many musical possibilities. Pushing a string upward across the fretboard raises (sharpens) the pitch of that note.

Learning to bend is all about knowing how far to push a string to get the note you want.

The Golden Rules for String-Bending

1. Support the finger that's doing the bend. If you're bending with your 1st finger then there's not a lot you can do. But if you bend with your 2nd, put the 1st down as well on the fret preceding, so you can push with both.

If you're bending with the 3rd finger, put the 1st and the 2nd down on the preceding frets and push with all three. This helps to stabilise your hand and give strength.

2. Avoid bending with your little finger. It isn't very strong.

3. If you want to bend a note on the 5th or 6th string, pull it down towards the floor.

4. Bends go better with light-gauge strings (0.009 sets).

5. Try putting your thumb over the neck to get more grip. The thumb position in the middle of the back of the neck (which you would use for barré chords) is no good for bending.

Also, don't let the lower strings slide on top of the fingernail of the finger that's doing the bend. Let them 'bunch' at the tip of the finger.

There are three main bends. We can raise the note D to E♭ (the half bend), to E (the one or full bend), and to F (the one and a half). The last one is hard and tends to break strings!

All three feature in Example 13+14.

(The '*8va*' sign means play the notes one octave higher than they are written here.)

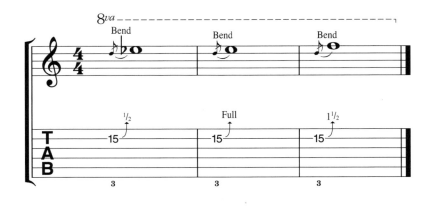

Don't worry if it takes a while to gauge how far to push. Bending accurately is a real skill, demanding a good ear and a sensitive left hand.

The next exercise offers a way of checking your pitch.

The first note in each bar is fretted and is the note you're aiming at with the bend. You then try and reach it with a bend.

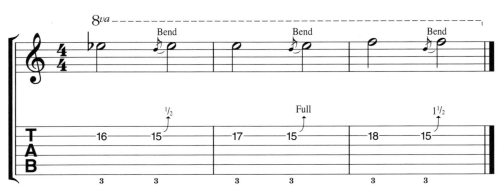

Vibrato

The last expressive technique we need to look at is vibrato, or 'finger-tremolo'. It's an effect created by a rapid alteration and restoration of pitch.

Singers use it very often to give colour to sustained notes. On the guitar it actually helps to prolong a note. At a sufficiently high volume, or with a lot of distortion, vibrato will sustain a note for as long as your left hand can stand.

You do it by pushing the string up and down a small distance – say a quarter of an inch – turning the left wrist rapidly back and forth.

The finger does a little of the movement, but most of it comes from the wrist. Grasp the neck firmly and put your thumb over it.

TRACKS 17+18

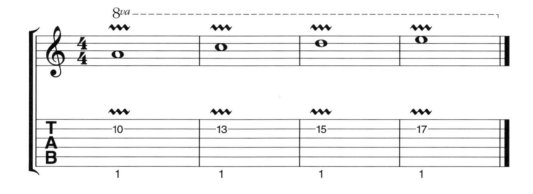

Although the lead phrases in this book give plenty of scope for vibrato the effect has not been notated. This is to keep things simple.

Try putting it in as you feel more confident, especially on the longer notes.

With the pull-off, hammer-on, slide, bend and vibrato, we're now properly equipped to go places.

Putting bends into the pentatonic minor scale is a bit like adding fuel-injection. Suddenly the thing is growling! Try these:

TRACKS 19+20

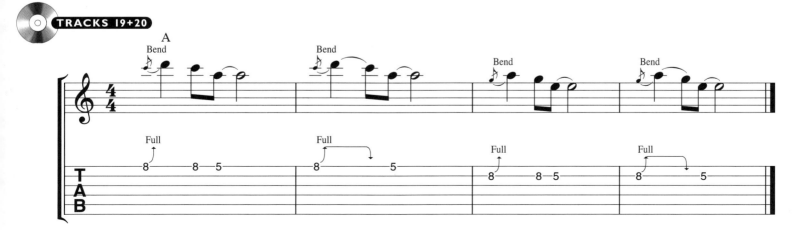

▶▶ MIKE RUTHERFORD (GENESIS)
"At first everything I write I think is brilliant!
Then a month later I listen to it, and I think that half of it's no good."

You notice the difference in sound between the second note in bars 1 and 2? In bar 1 the bend came down to C and the C was hit by the right hand. In bar 2 the bend came down to C but the C wasn't struck. The release of the bend itself produced the note.

Bends can be really 'worked' to get the most out of them. In the next example bend up to the first note and stay there, hitting it four times before releasing it and hitting G at the 8th fret.

In bar 2 you do the same thing except the G is created just by the string being allowed to come down. It's a subtle but significant difference.

You always have this option. Notice how bar 3 is a full bend and bar 4 only a half bend.

TRACKS 21+22

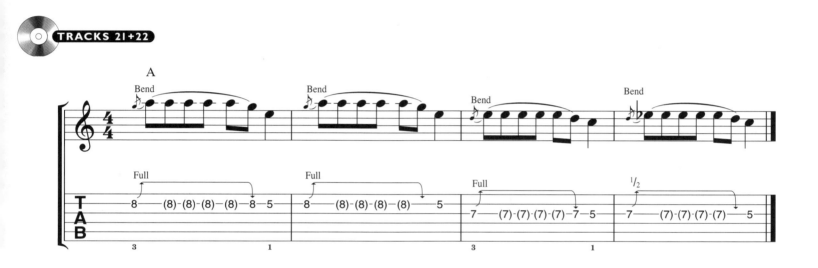

The contrast between the full and the half bend is important. Here's another chance to practise it:

TRACKS 23+24

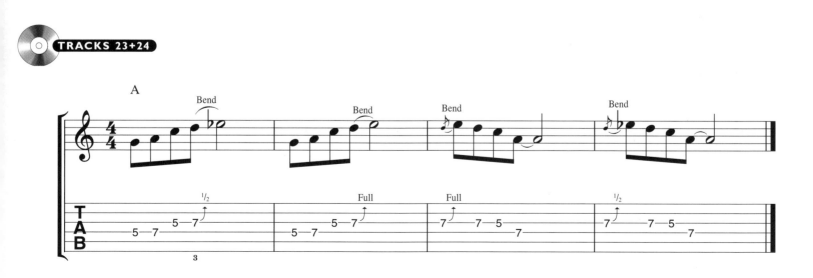

Here's a way of using the scale that creates surprise. The hammer-on stays the same for much of it but the higher note is changing.

TRACKS 25+26

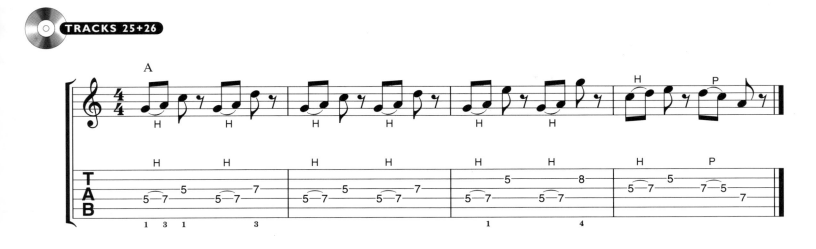

Since the pentatonic scale has only got five notes, it doesn't take very long to go up and down.

So how do we get more from it? Here's one idea: the extended hammer-on/pull-off.

TRACKS 27+28

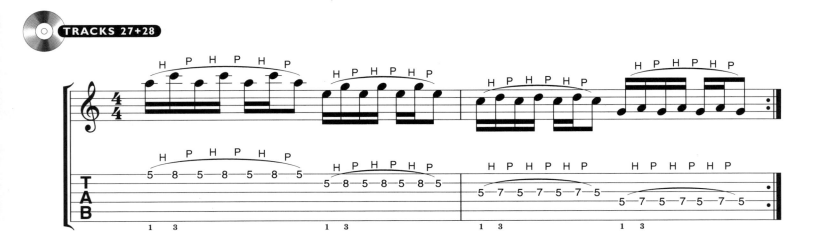

Another way of extending the scale is to come down it playing 3 or 4 notes at a time and then going back a couple. I think of this as 'doubling back':

TRACKS 29+30

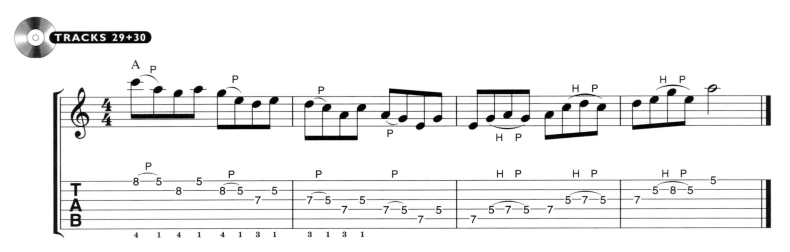

First Mile

Now it's time to use some of these ideas in an eight-bar solo.

We're playing over an A–D chord change but you don't need to take that too much into account because the pentatonic minor won't clash horribly with the D chord.

TRACKS 31+32

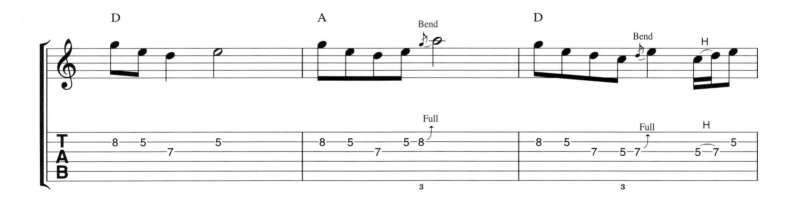

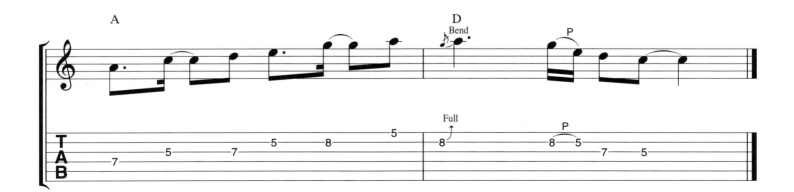

CHARLOTTE CAFFEY (THE GO-GO'S)

Out Of Town

It's important to think about your phrasing – how you shape your selection of notes. One way to do this is through repetition.

Notice how, in Example 31+32, the first three notes of bars 1–4 use the same rhythm. The same idea occurs in our next eight-bar break. For the sake of a contrast, after playing eighth notes for much of bars 1–4, bars 5–6 have fewer notes.

Remember, you don't have to keep playing constantly – an endless stream of notes gets boring very quickly. The dots above the notes in bar 7 indicate they should be played in a 'clipped' ('staccato') manner, with almost no sustain.

To get this effect put your pick against the 3rd string immediately after you hit each note:

TRACKS 33+34

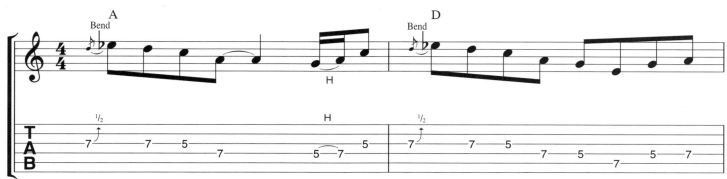

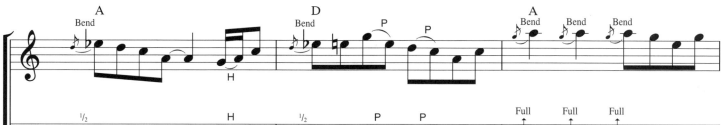

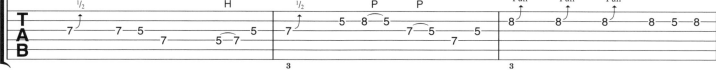

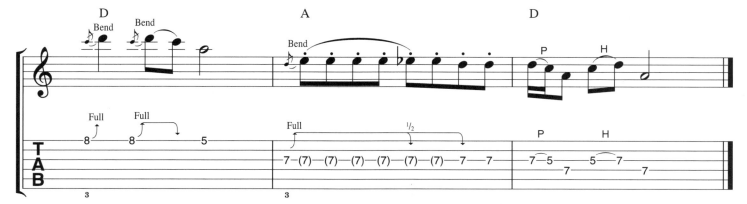

The next two examples use the extension to the pentatonic given in Example 3+4.

In Example 37+38 bends are combined with a quick hammer-on/pull-off. On the second beat you have three sixteenth notes (semiquavers) played on the beat and followed by a single eighth note. This is a common phrase:

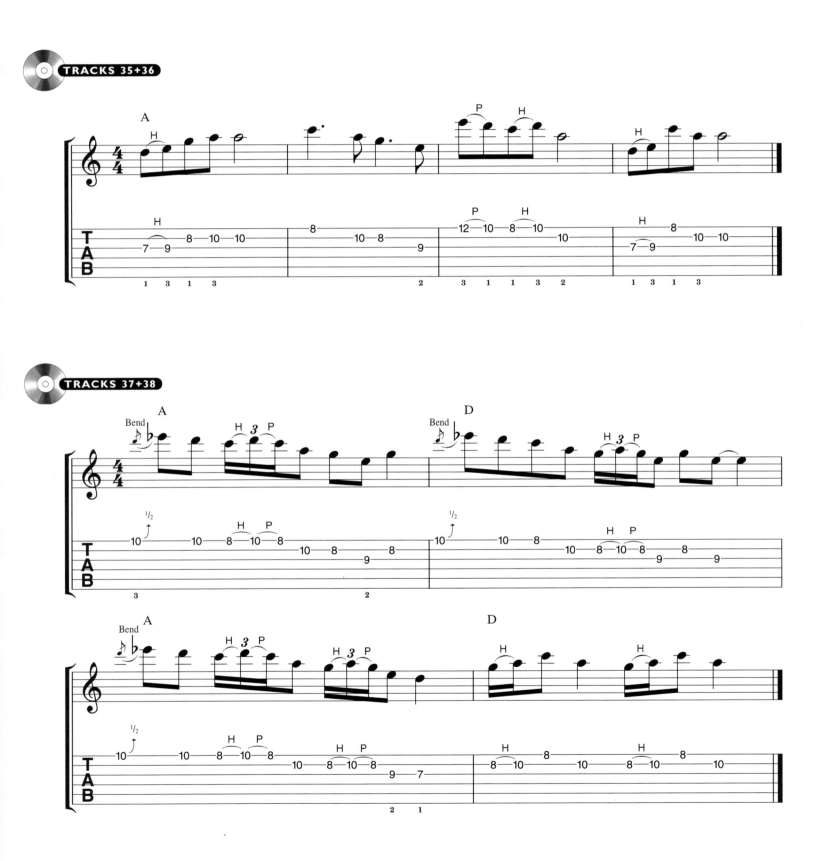

Changing Gear
Playing In The Open Position

The notes of the pentatonic minor scale can be found all over the neck. Let's look at some other places where we can find them. Here they are in 1st position using open strings.

Note that this does not start on the root note A.

A is the third note of the pattern:

TRACKS 39+40

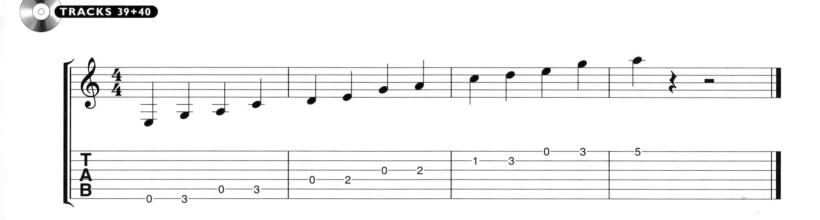

This is useful when we want some low notes to contrast with phrases played higher.

The open strings make hammer-ons and pull-offs readily available:

TRACKS 41+42

▶▶ JIMI HENDRIX
"...music is gonna be here, regardless if it's rock or whatever, you know, and it's gonna influence a whole lotta people's minds now, because like I said before, that's part of their church now."

Good solos often feature an element of surprise.
There are many ways to do this. One is to
change direction and use a wide interval.

In bar 1 of Example 43+44 you drop from G
to C and rise to A. The C has a microtone bend.

This is a bend smaller than a semitone
(written as 1/4). Microtone bends give a solo a
blues feel. Bar 4 is a more intricate pull-off
and slide phrase:

TRACKS 43+44

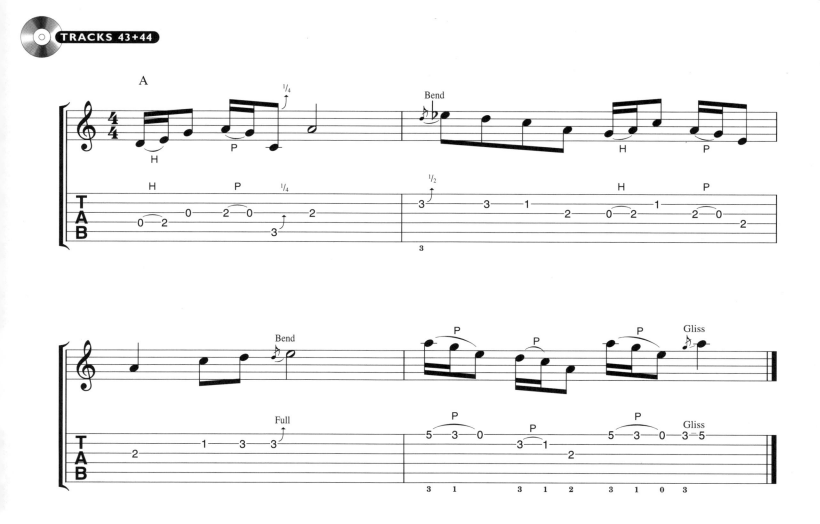

Stepping Free
Part 1

Here are two further eight-bar breaks using this lower pentatonic scale position. We're now playing over A and G, so the notes G and D tend to be emphasised when the chord changes to G in bars 3 and 7.

This is a simple example of the lead being aware of the harmony. Example 45+46 uses quite a bit of sustain. Listen out for the high G in bar 5 struck whilst you've bent D up to E on the 2nd string.

TRACKS 45+46

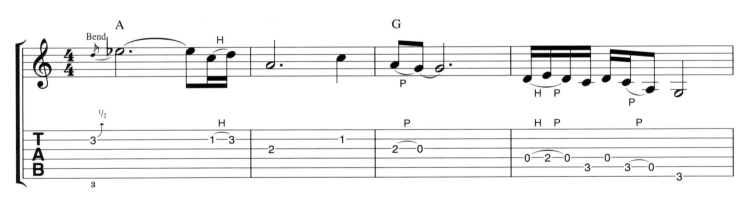

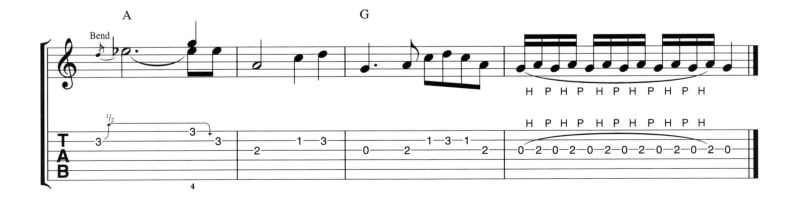

Stepping Free
Part 2

Here we move from 1st position to the 5th fret area and then further up. This low-to-high phrasing is a classic way of building to a climax.

TRACKS 47+48

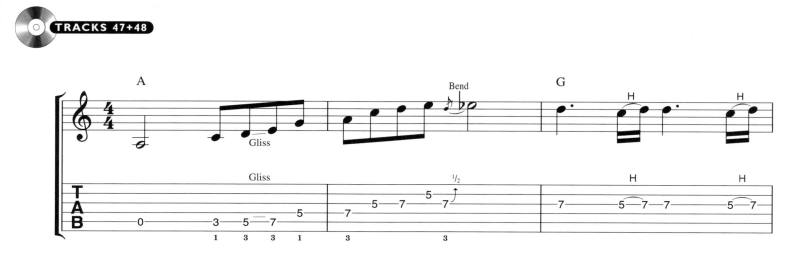

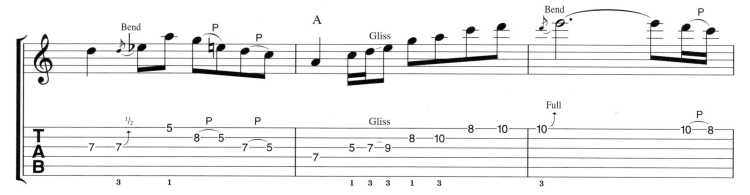

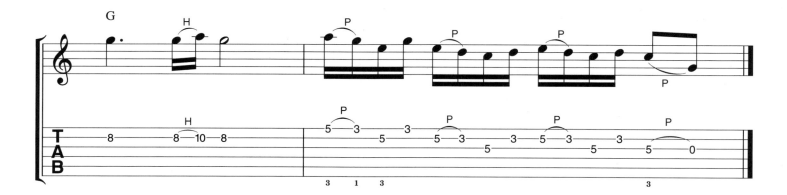

Pedal To The Floor
Playing Above The 12th Fret

Now it's time to venture to the 12th fret and beyond in search of those fierce, wailing notes that are so closely associated with rock lead guitar.

The next scale pattern gives us the pentatonic minor up to the 17th fret:

TRACKS 49+50

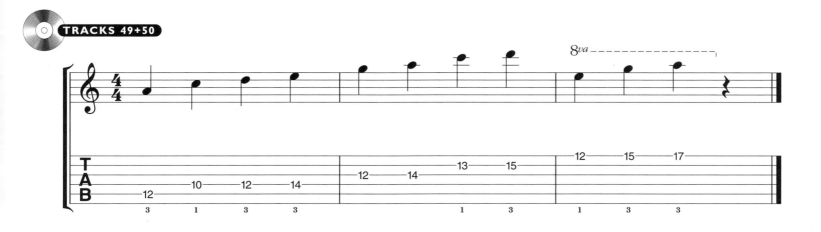

Here's a phrase built on this pattern. It starts on the 4th beat of the bar, so you hear three clicks and then the first notes.

Watch out for the first bend – pull the string down.

TRACKS 51+52

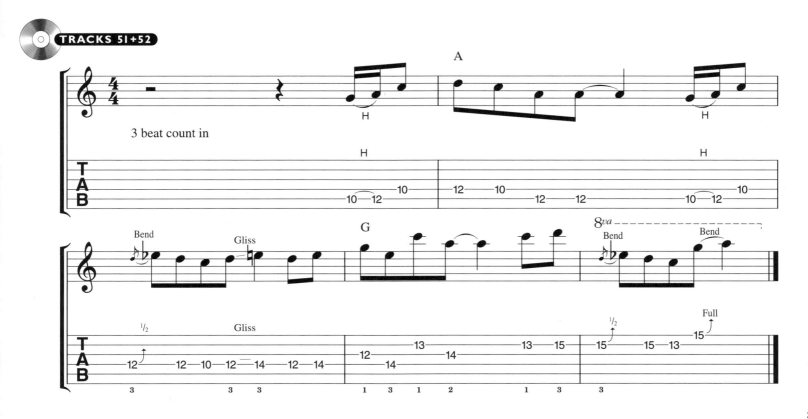

This next break works in the opposite direction.
Watch out for the bend on the first finger in
bar 3 and the quick sixteenth note pull-off in
bar 4 where you need to deploy your little finger.

TRACKS 53+54

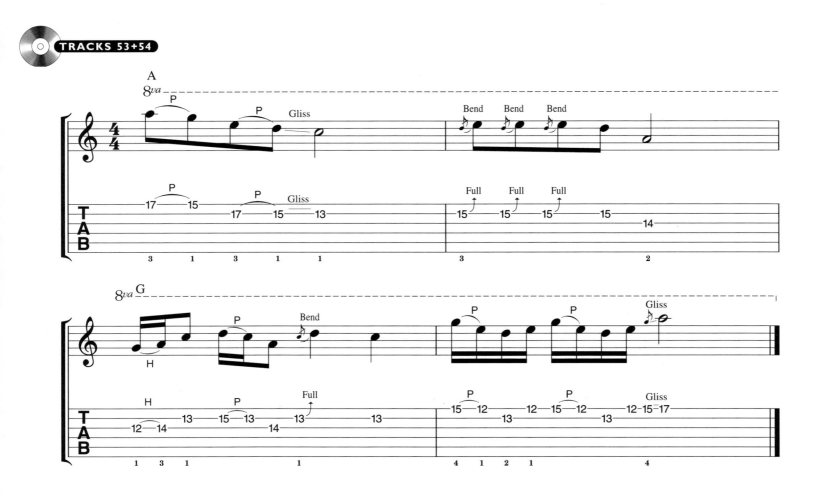

Our last pentatonic minor pattern is in fact
Example 1+2 moved up 12 frets.

Remember: add 12 to any position to get the
same phrase/scale/chord an octave higher.

TRACKS 55+56

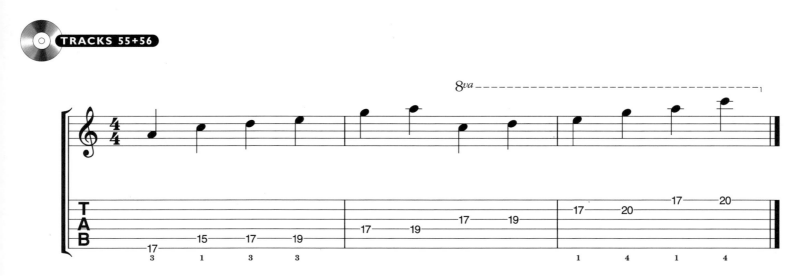

Here are the definitive bends on this scale, where the guitar can really scream. Once you get steady with the bends, try adding vibrato.

Shake your finger and wrist, close your eyes — instant late '60s English rock/blues!

TRACKS 57+58

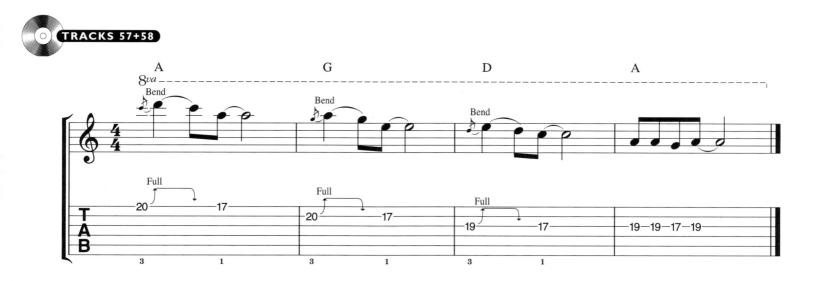

The opening of the next example is probably the most famous rock lead lick of them all:

TRACKS 59+60

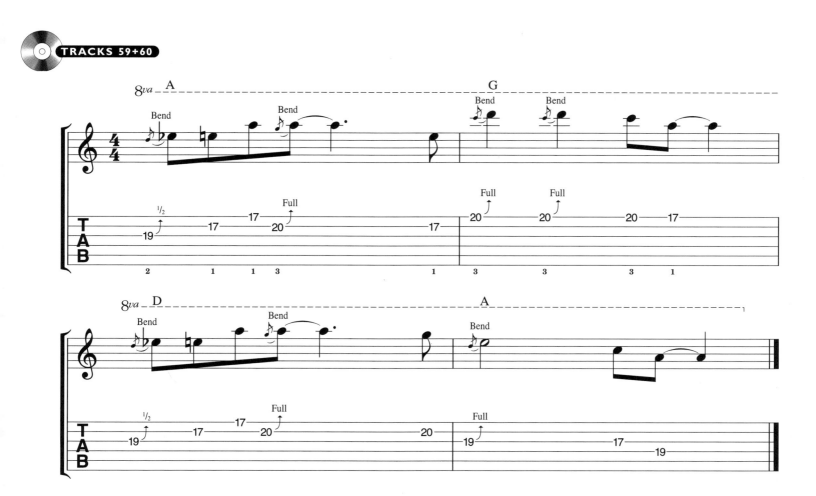

▶▶ *BRIAN MAY*
"I use coins instead of a plectrum because they're not flexible.
I think you get more control if all the flexing is due to the movement in your fingers.
You get better contact with the strings, and depending on how tightly you hold it,
you have total control over how hard it's being played, and because of its round surface
and the serration, by turning it different ways you can get different sounds..."

Horizon

Here's an eight-bar solo that goes from low
to high. You'll see four definite shifts of position.

TRACKS 61+62

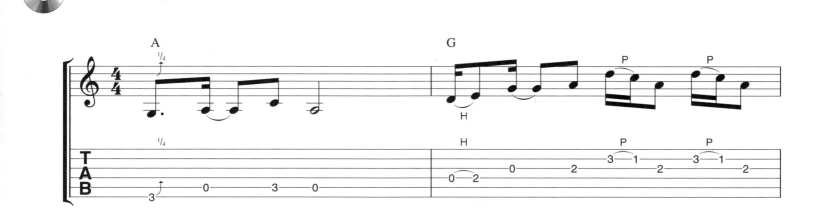

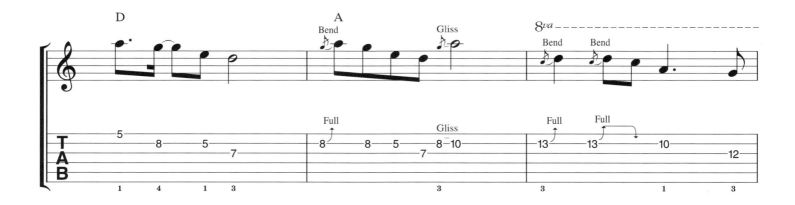

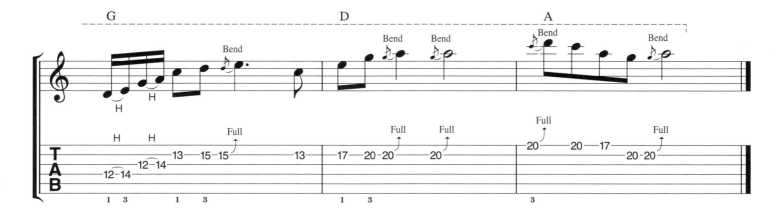

One Particular Place To Go
Chuck Berry Style Licks

We've looked at the pentatonic minor because it's so popular and flexible. Knowing which chord sequences you can play it over is a complex matter, partly depending on experience and taste.

Let's just say you can use it safely in the major key – in this case A major – if the backing uses major chords named after the notes of the scale: A C D E G. That's if you want that tough sound. If the backing uses the three minor chords that belong to the key – in this case Bm, C♯m and F♯m – the risk of a horrible 'wrong' note rises dramatically. You may need to use another type of scale which we'll be looking at later.

But there's more than one way of travelling. One useful vehicle that most rock guitarists roll affectionately out of the garage every now and then is a bunch of licks made famous by Chuck Berry.

As classic as a '50s Chevrolet, here's the first: the unison bend. Bend D to E on the 3rd string and then hit E on the 2nd. You then do the same thing on the 2nd and 1st strings.

Make sure that 3rd finger is supported by your 2nd.

TRACKS 63+64

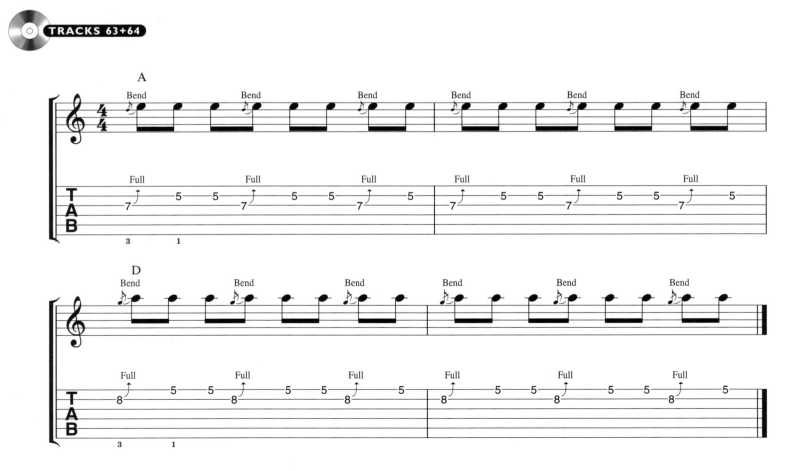

▶▶ FastForward™
Guide To Guitar

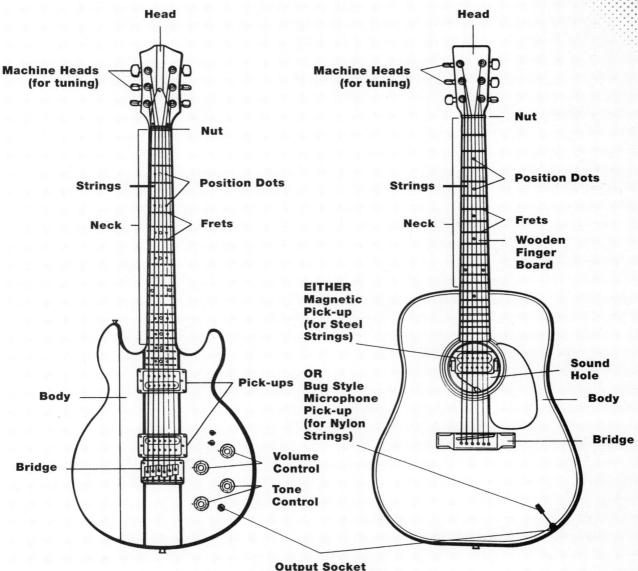

Head

Machine Heads
(for tuning)

Nut

Strings

Position Dots

Neck

Frets

Body

Pick-ups

Bridge

EITHER
Magnetic
Pick-up
(for Steel
Strings)

OR
Bug Style
Microphone
Pick-up
(for Nylon
Strings)

Volume
Control

Tone
Control

Output Socket
(to audio amplifier)

Head

Machine Heads
(for tuning)

Nut

Strings

Position Dots

Neck

Frets

Wooden
Finger
Board

Sound
Hole

Body

Bridge

Pull-Out Chart

The Guitar

Whether you have an acoustic or an electric guitar, the principles of playing are fundamentally the same, and so are most of the features on both instruments.

In order to 'electrify' an acoustic guitar (as in the diagram), a magnetic pick up can be attached to those guitars with steel strings or a 'bug' style microphone pick-up can be attached to guitars with nylon strings.

If in doubt check with your local music shop.

Tuning Your Guitar

Tuning
Accurate tuning of the guitar is essential, and is achieved by winding the machine heads up or down. It is always better to 'tune up' to the correct pitch rather than down.

Therefore, if you find that the pitch of your string is higher (sharper) than the correct pitch, you should 'wind down' below the correct pitch, and then 'tune up' to it.

Relative Tuning
Tuning the guitar to itself without the aid of a pitch pipe or other tuning device.

Other Methods Of Tuning
Pitch pipe
Tuning fork
Dedicated electronic guitar tuner

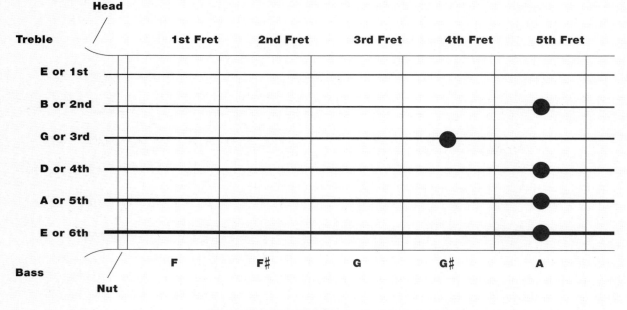

 Press down where indicated, one at a time, following the instructions below.

Estimate the pitch of the 6th string as near as possible to **E** or at least a comfortable pitch (not too high or you might break other strings in tuning up).

Then, while checking the various positions on the above diagram, place a finger from your left hand on:

• The 5th fret of the E or 6th string and **tune the open A** (or 5th string) to the note (A)

• The 5th fret of the A or 5th string and **tune the open D** (or 4th string) to the note (D)

• The 5th fret of the D or 4th string and **tune the open G** (or 3rd string) to the note (G)

• The 4th fret of the G or 3rd string and **tune the open B** (or 2nd string) to the note (B)

• The 5th fret of the B or 2nd string and **tune the open E** (or 1st string) to the note (E)

Chord Boxes

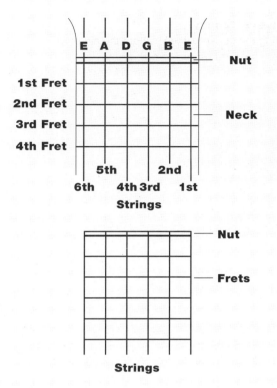

Nut

Neck

1st Fret
2nd Fret
3rd Fret
4th Fret

E A D G B E

5th   2nd
6th 4th 3rd 1st
Strings

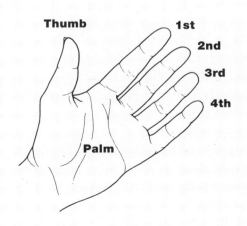

Nut

Frets

Strings

The A Chord

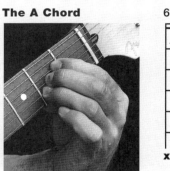

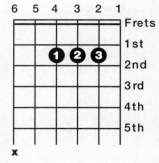

6 5 4 3 2 1

Frets
1st
2nd
3rd
4th
5th

x

x = do not play this string

Chord boxes are diagrams of the guitar neck viewed head upwards, face on, as illustrated in the above drawings. The horizontal double line at the top is the nut, the other horizontal lines are the frets. The vertical lines are the strings starting from E or 6th on the left to E or 1st on the right.

Any dots with numbers inside them simply indicate which finger goes where. Any strings marked with an **x** must not be played.

The fingers of your hand are numbered 1, 2, 3, & 4 as in the diagram below.

Thumb **1st**
2nd
3rd
4th
Palm

All chords are major chords unless otherwise indicated.

Left Hand
Place all three fingers into position and press down firmly. Keep your thumb around the middle of the back of the neck and directly behind your 1st and 2nd fingers.

Right Hand Thumb Or Plectrum
Slowly play each string, starting with the 5th or A string and moving up to the 1st or E string.

If there is any buzzing, perhaps you need to:-
Position your fingers nearer the metal fret (towards you); or adjust the angle of your hand; or check that the buzz is not elsewhere on the guitar by playing the open strings in the same manner.

Finally, your nails may be too long, in which case you are pressing down at an extreme angle and therefore not firmly enough. Also the pad of one of your fingers may be in the way of the next string for the same reason.

So, cut your nails to a more comfortable length and then try to keep them as near vertical to the fretboard as possible.

Once you have a 'buzz-free' sound, play the chord a few times and then remove your fingers and repeat the exercise until your positioning is right instinctively.

Holding The Guitar

The picture above shows a comfortable position for playing rock or pop guitar

The Right Hand
When STRUMMING (brushing your fingers across the strings), hold your fingers together.

When PICKING (plucking strings individually), hold your wrist further away from the strings than for strumming.

Keep your thumb slightly to the left of your fingers which should be above the three treble strings as shown.

The Plectrum
Many modern guitar players prefer to use a plectrum to strike the strings. Plectrums come in many sizes, shapes and thicknesses and are available from your local music shop.

Start with a fairly large, soft one if possible, with a grip. The photo shows the correct way to hold your plectrum.

The Left Hand
Use your fingertips to press down on the strings in the positions described. Your thumb should be behind your 1st and 2nd fingers pressing on the middle of the back of the neck.

RM92051G

Here it is souped-up with the addition of an
extra note for a fatter sound:

TRACKS 65+66

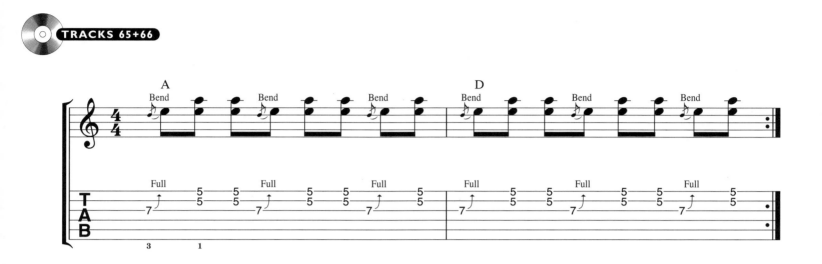

Unison bends hit simultaneously are
handy whenever you want to stress a phrase.
In the next example you're playing the root
notes of a D E G A chord sequence.

Listen for how they 'mesh' with the backing:

TRACKS 67+68

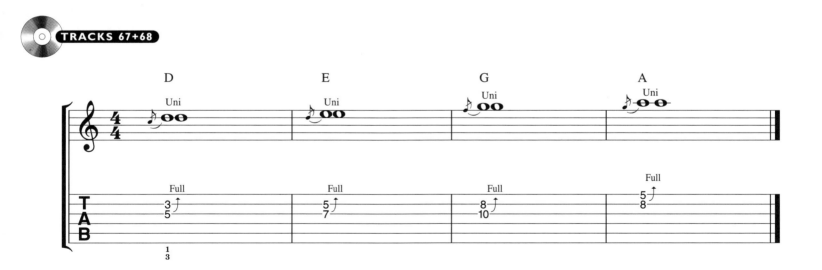

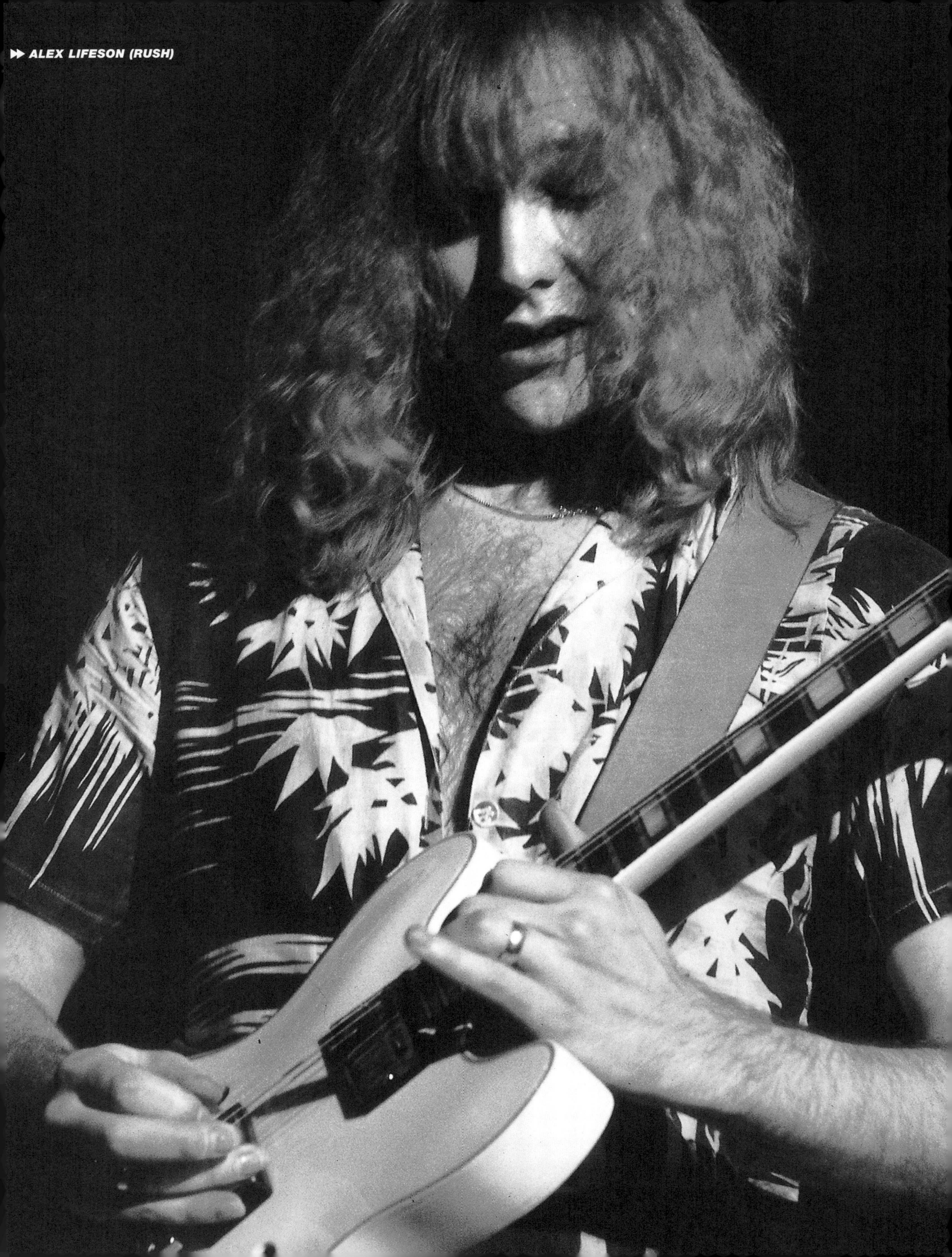

If the next lick doesn't make you want to
duckwalk across your living room, nothing will.
Listen for the syncopated rhythm in bar 2:
the notes are held across the bar line.

This suggests that good time rock'n'roll groove:

TRACKS 69+70

How about an extra touch of chrome?
Just add a strategically-placed C#:

TRACKS 71+72

Here's another classic lick. Feel the pauses
between the stabbing notes.

The interval between the notes on the top two
strings is called a fourth:

TRACKS 73+74

3½ beats count in

This style of lead often begins with a slide of
two notes:

TRACKS 75+76

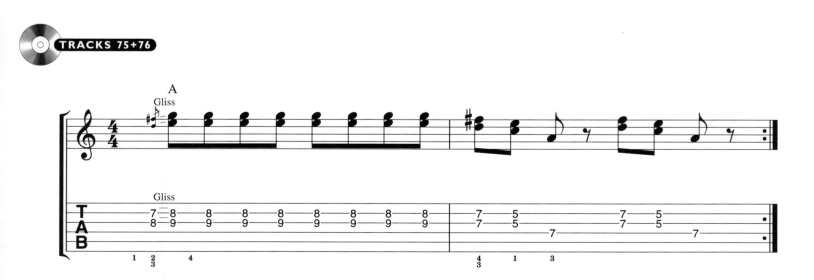

Instead of hitting these notes together we
can also play them one after the other and let
them blur.

Bars 3–4 are famous. The notes at the 7th fret
can be played with just the 3rd finger.

TRACKS 77+78

▶▶ *CHUCK BERRY*
"The feeling to harmonize began to be a desire of mine; to get away from the normal melody and add my own melody and harmony was imperial, and I guess that grew into the appreciation for music."

Hubcap Lipstick

Over a backing of A and D played in a
rock'n'roll style, let's play an eight-bar break,
putting some of these licks together.

Watch out for the open E in bar 3. We could
have fretted it on the 2nd string at the 5th fret,

but using the open string enables you to
take all your fingers off and get them ready for
the next bar.

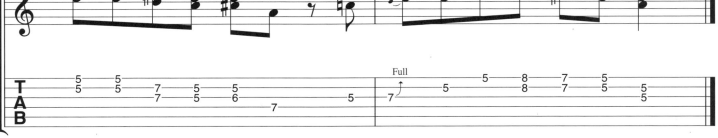

TRACKS 79+80

Travelling In Style
The Major Pentatonic Scale

We tore it up with the pentatonic minor, and we've duckwalked with some '50s rock lead. Now let's learn a scale that will enable us to play over all the chords – major and minor – of a major key. We'll start in first position:

TRACKS 81+82

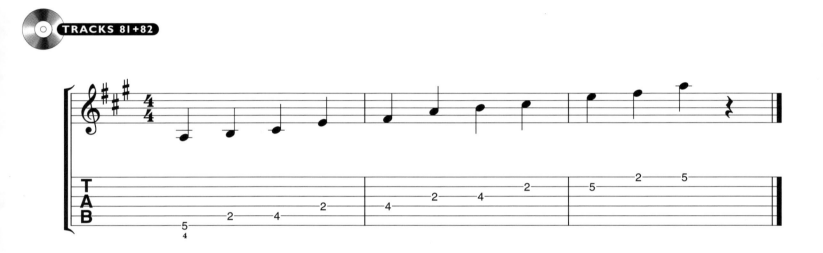

This is the scale of A pentatonic major. It has five notes – A B C♯ E F♯ – all taken from the full major scale. The three sharp signs on the stave tell you all the Fs Cs Gs are played sharp unless a natural sign (♮) cancels out the sharp.

This is the key signature of A major. Here's an extended fingering:

TRACKS 83+84

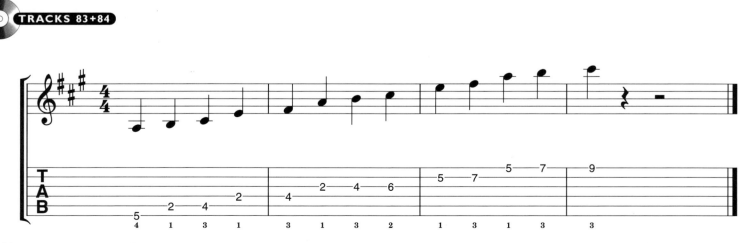

As a major scale, this expresses a different range of emotions than the pentatonic minor.

If your chord sequence will allow it, they can be combined within a single lead break – but that's another drive for another day.

You'll notice it sounds more upbeat and less bluesy.

Try these phrases around the lower position. Watch out for the low bend on the 1st finger in bar 2.

TRACKS 85+86

Here are the most useful bends on this scale position:

TRACKS 87+88

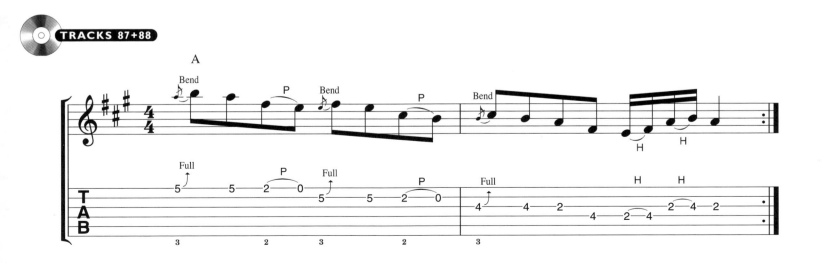

► **KEITH RICHARDS**
"There's really only one song in the whole world, and probably Adam and Eve hummed it to each other, and everything else is variation on it in some form or another, you know."

Now let's shift from low to a bit higher.
Hear how the bends in bar 3 give a swing to the
playing:

TRACKS 89+90

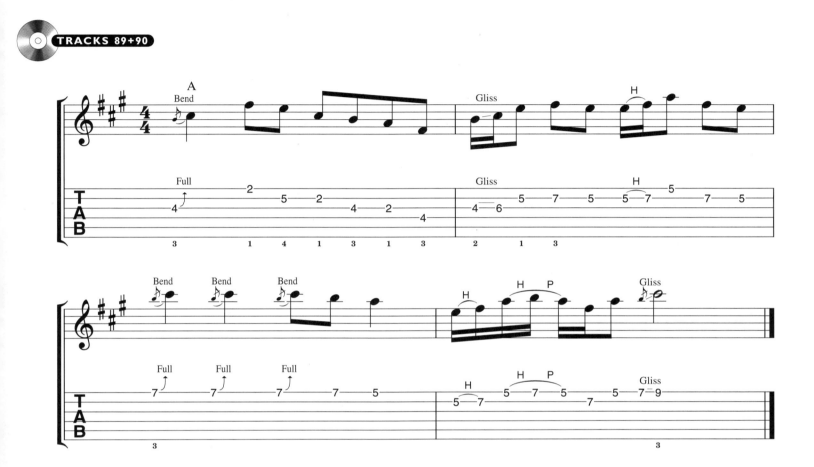

A higher position for the scale invites a
change of gear:

TRACKS 91+92

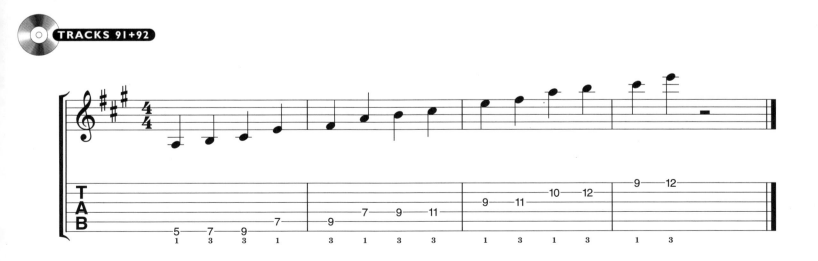

There's something about the sound of this scale that just invites your fingers to slide back and forth between the notes. Bars 1–2 are repeated an octave higher for 3–4:

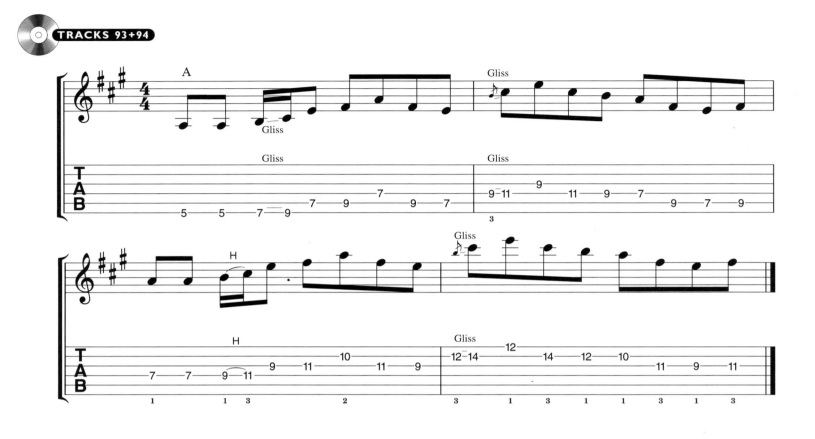

Try this four-bar phrase to get the hang of the changing positions. Each bar is placed at a different point on the neck, although they're all using the same notes:

One For The Road

Here's an eight-bar solo played over a chord sequence that mixes major and minor chords (as most songs do). Just as an experiment try playing a pentatonic minor break over the track.

The result is likely to sound either peculiar, very odd, or downright horrible depending on which notes of the scale you choose to play.

By contrast, the major pentatonic notes glide across this sequence like a dream.

Watch out for the 1st finger bend in bar 5:

TRACKS 97+98

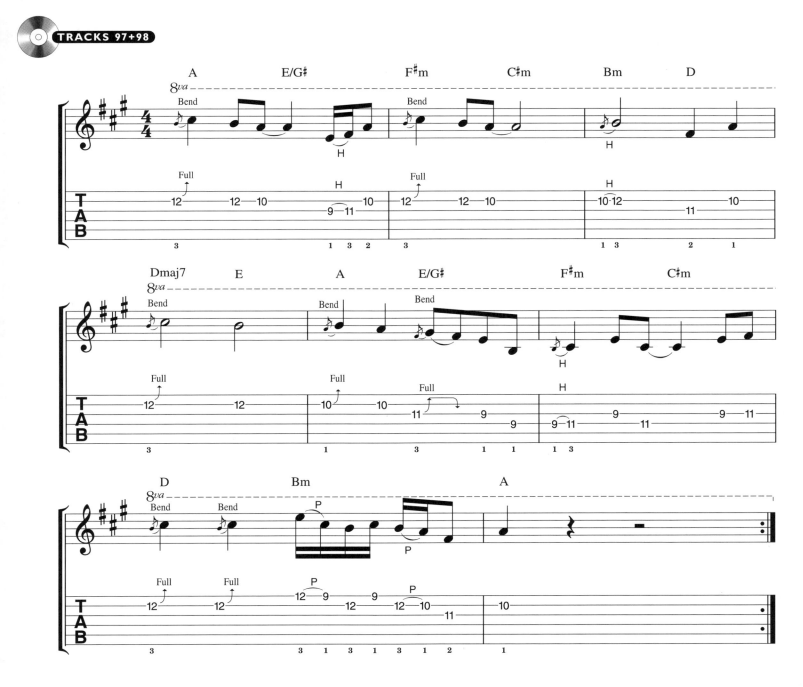

▶▶ FRANK ZAPPA
"I figured the only way I was going to get to hear enough of what I wanted to hear was to get an instrument and play it myself."

Oh Chevrolet!
An Extended Solo

To finish, here's a more extended guitar solo which draws on many of the ideas that we've tried out in this book. *'Oh Chevrolet!'* is structured in three parts:

Section 1: (bars 1–17). Allowing for the one bar pick-up, this is a 16-bar block using a four-bar chord sequence four times.
The chord sequence is A G D A D C.

Section 2: (bars 18–25). An eight-bar phrase changing E D A.

Section 3: (bars 26–43). Another 16-bar block, this time starting with an F♯m D E sequence three times, and then a return to the A G D of section 1.

Section 1

The key of 'Oh Chevrolet!' is A major (A B C♯ D E F♯ G♯ A). If you compare the rhythm chords (A G D A D C) with the notes of the A pentatonic minor scale (A C D E G), you'll notice that they match. So it's safe to play either A pentatonic minor or major lead phrases.

The pentatonic minor phrases are easy to spot on the notation, you just have to look for C natural (C♮) or G natural (G♮).

Here's how the solo is put together:

Bar 1: The first phrase comes in on the 2nd offbeat. Count 1 2 3 4 1 2 AND. That's where you hit the first note. Notice the solo starts low down.

Bar 2: To play the glissando, put your finger on the 12th fret of the lowest string, strike the note and slide it downwards.

Bar 3: Listen to the distinctive slurring effect of the C and C♯ coming after each other, also the way the G and F♯ fit the chord change.

Bar 4: For contrast, a descending pentatonic major run. Watch out for the last note tied into the next bar.

Bar 5: This is a copy of bar 3 with the last two notes changed to fit the chords D C.

Bar 6: This starts as pentatonic major but the bends go only up a ½ tone, to C, which is the pentatonic minor.

Bar 7: The first four notes mimic bar 4, but the second group are the pentatonic minor and establish the first change of position (to the 5th fret).

Bars 8–9: Staying with the E♭ bend creates a pause in the music. You don't have to play all the time.

Bar 10: The last four notes are the same as bar 1 but an octave higher.

Bar 11: A standard bend, but the last note of each four is G first time, F♯ second time.

Bars 12–13: This phrase uses a ½ tone bend to move from a pentatonic major note (F♯) to a minor one (G). Watch out for the tie across the bar-line.

Bars 14–15: These mimic 12–13 by keeping a similar rhythm and bend and moving it onto the top string.

Bars 16–17: We're now at the end of the first section so we want to create a sense of anticipation for what's coming next. One way to do this is to play a sequence of unison bends. They also have the result of moving us to the 12th fret — another position change.

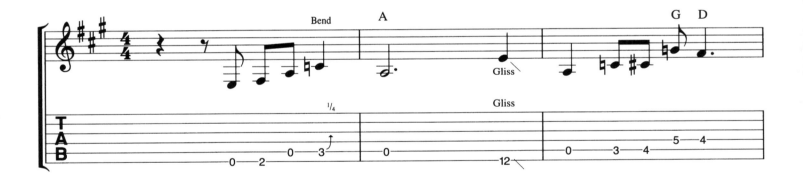

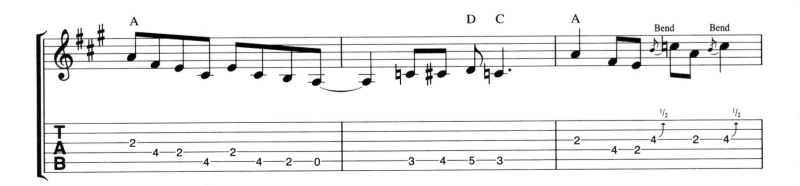

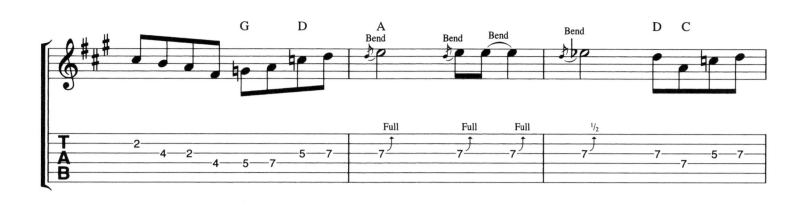

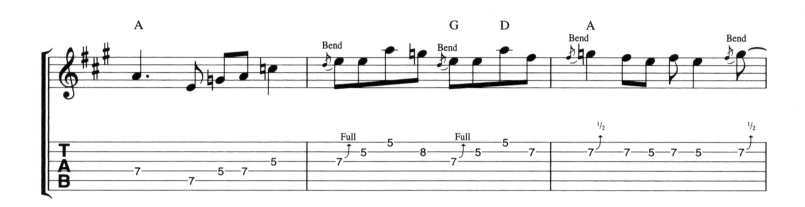

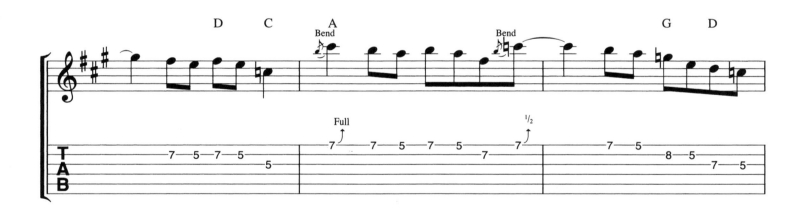

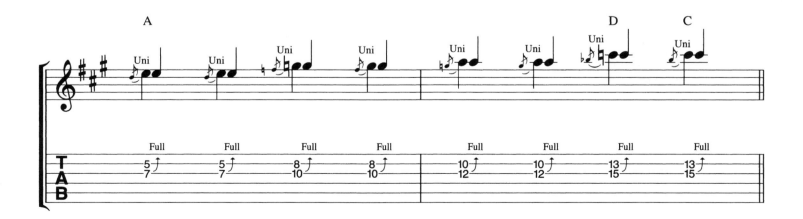

▶▶ *KURT COBAIN*

Section 2

Bar 18: The backing chord is E. We change to an E pentatonic minor run, giving a bluesy effect. The last note F leads to the F♯ of the next bar.

Bar 19: The backing goes down from E to D, one tone. So we play the same run as in bar 18 but 2 frets lower (D pentatonic minor). The last note C links to the C♯ in the next bar.

Bar 20: The backing chord is now A and we're back at the 5th fret. This is the same run again simply transposed to A.

Bar 21: Bend up, let down and pull-off onto the C natural.

Bars 22–24: These use the Chuck Berry-style double-stop lick from Part Five. You simply move it to wherever the chord is; here, that means frets 12, 10 and 5.

Bar 25: The section finishes with a downward run to the lowest A, giving a feeling that some form of end has been reached.

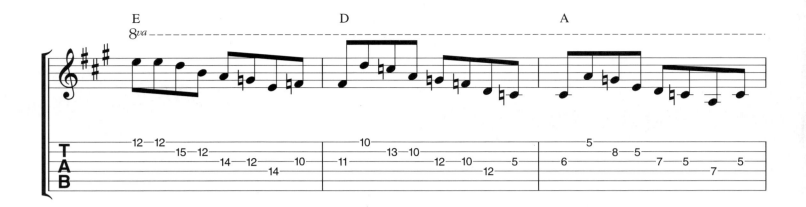

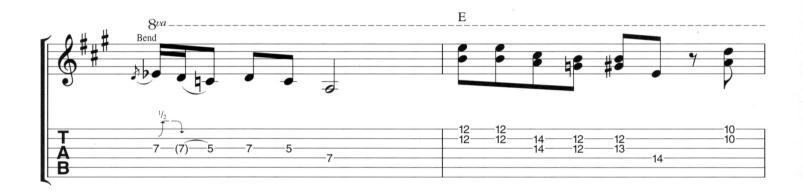

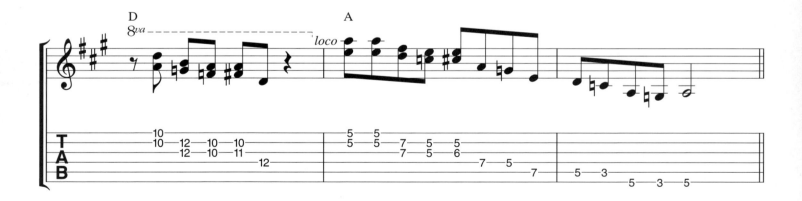

▶▶ DAVE NAVARRO (JANE'S ADDICTION & THE RED HOT CHILI PEPPERS)

Section 3

Bar 26–27: The backing takes on more of a minor feel for the next 12 bars. Accordingly we shift to F♯ pentatonic minor.

Bar 28: For a slightly different tone, we can use some open strings.

Bar 29: This echoes the bend in bar 27.

Bars 30–31: The open A string in bar 30 gives us a moment where the left hand isn't tied to the fretboard to make a change of position, continuing the run up from the 7th fret.

Bars 32–33: These are chord based phrases, the first on D simply played two frets higher for the E chord.

Bars 34–35: Two phrases using typical 'screaming' bends. This is the F♯ pentatonic minor scale at the 14th fret.

Bars 36–37: This minor-oriented section ends with our highest bend.

Bars 38–39: This chord backing returns to an A pentatonic minor feel, so our lead changes accordingly. Notice the bluesier sound of this after the minor feel of the previous 12 bars.

Bars 40–41: The phrase in 41 is A pentatonic minor one octave above the common 5th fret position.

Bars 42–43: Bend the C slowly to C♯.

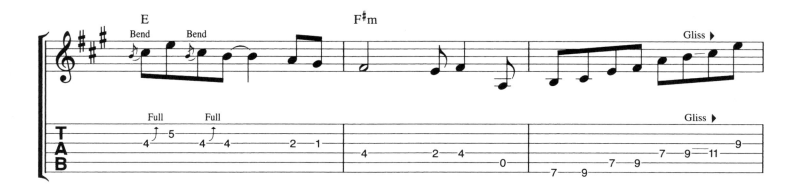

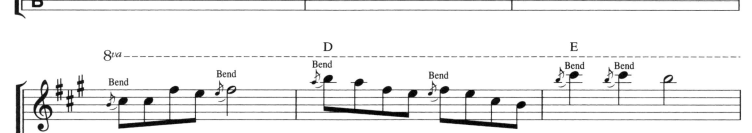

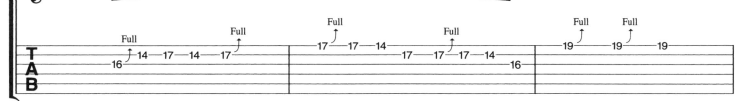

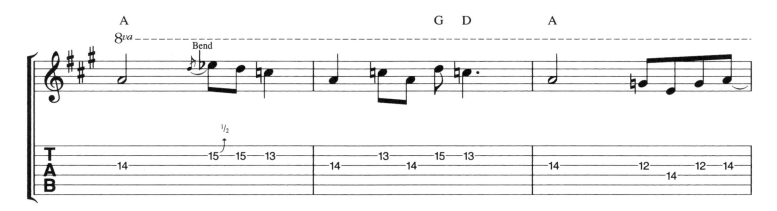

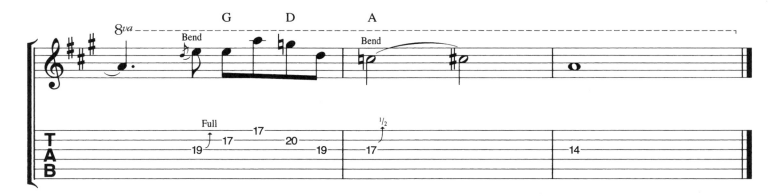

'Oh Chevrolet!' shows how phrasing and repetition are important. You don't have to keep coming up with phrases different to those you've already played.

Repeating a phrase helps your audience, because it gives them the pleasure of recognising something you've already played.

Notice also how a change of scale stops things becoming boring, and how it's important to take account of what the backing is doing.

This opens up a much bigger area of lead guitar playing which you'll be ready to approach when you're happy with the ideas we've looked at.

EASY   INTERMEDIATE   ADVANCED

Oh Chevrolet!

TRACKS 99+100

Section 1

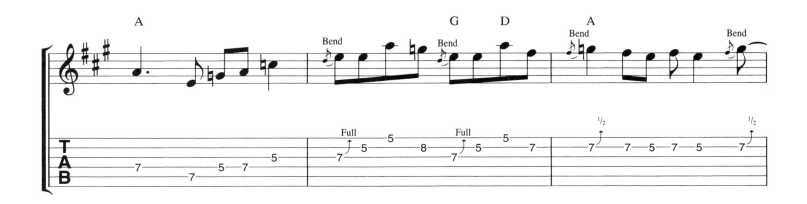

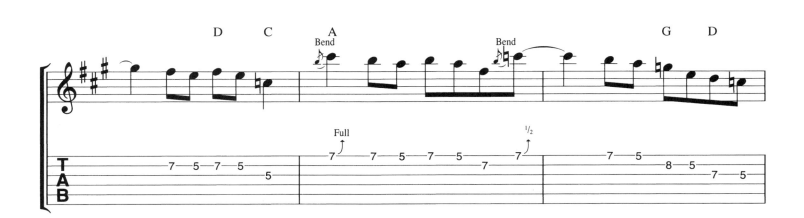

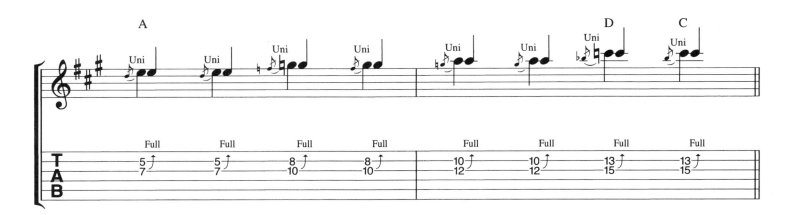

Section 2

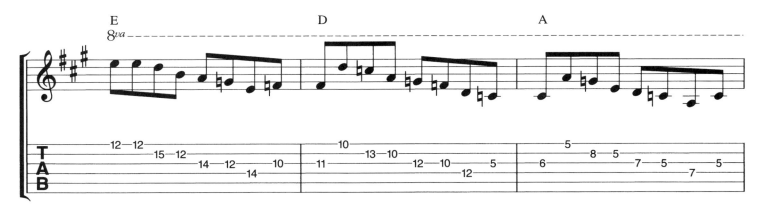

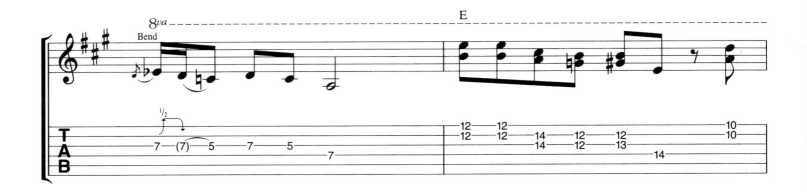

Section 3

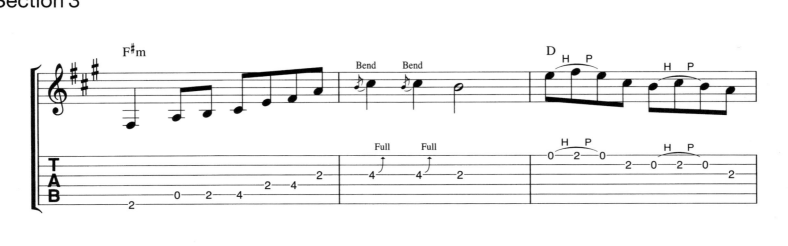

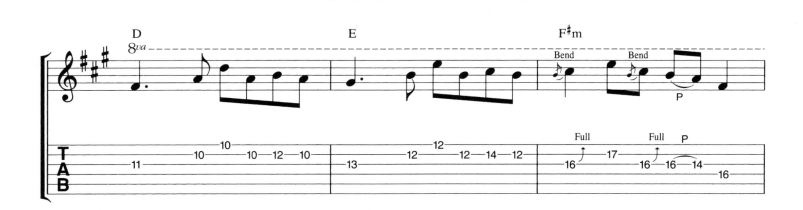

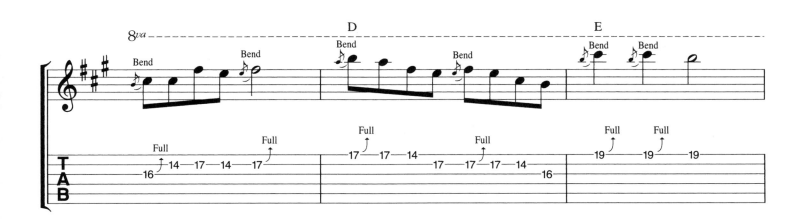

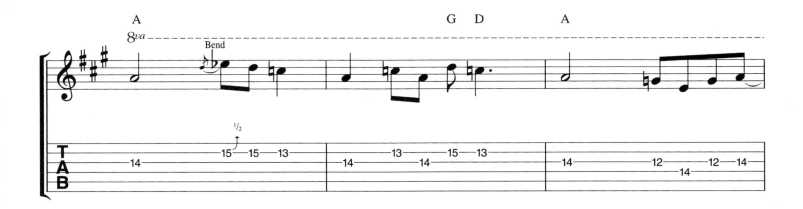

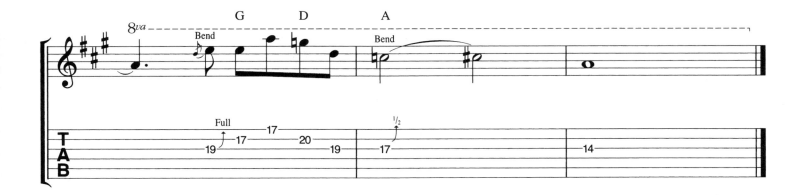

▶▶ *ERIC CLAPTON*

*"I hear a lot of my style in other guitar players.
The funny part is, the parts that I recognise as being directly taken from
my playing are the parts about my playing that I don't like.
Funny enough, what I like about my playing are still the parts that I copied."*

▶▶ *FastForward*™
Guide To Guitar

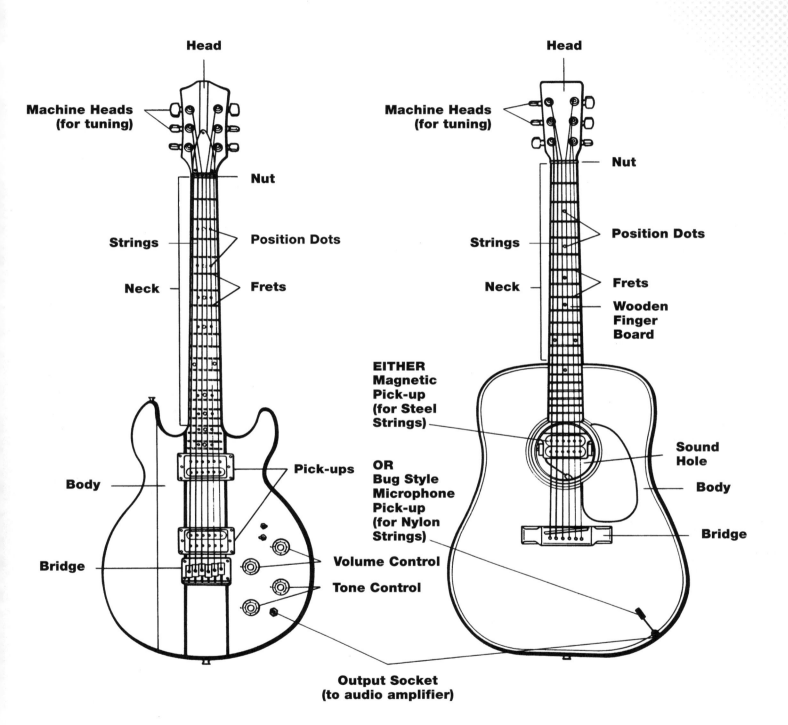

Head

Machine Heads (for tuning)

Nut

Strings

Position Dots

Neck

Frets

Body

Pick-ups

Bridge

Head

Machine Heads (for tuning)

Nut

Position Dots

Strings

Frets

Neck

Wooden Finger Board

EITHER Magnetic Pick-up (for Steel Strings)

OR Bug Style Microphone Pick-up (for Nylon Strings)

Sound Hole

Body

Bridge

Volume Control

Tone Control

Output Socket (to audio amplifier)

The Guitar

Whether you have an acoustic or an electric guitar, the principles of playing are fundamentally the same, and so are most of the features on both instruments.

In order to 'electrify' an acoustic guitar (as in the diagram), a magnetic pick up can be attached to those guitars with steel strings or a 'bug' style microphone pick-up can be attached to guitars with nylon strings.

If in doubt check with your local music shop.

Tuning Your Guitar

Tuning
Accurate tuning of the guitar is essential, and is achieved by winding the machine heads up or down. It is always better to 'tune up' to the correct pitch rather than down.

Therefore, if you find that the pitch of your string is higher (sharper) than the correct pitch, you should 'wind down' below the correct pitch, and then 'tune up' to it.

Relative Tuning
Tuning the guitar to itself without the aid of a pitch pipe or other tuning device.

Other Methods Of Tuning
Pitch pipe
Tuning fork
Dedicated electronic guitar tuner

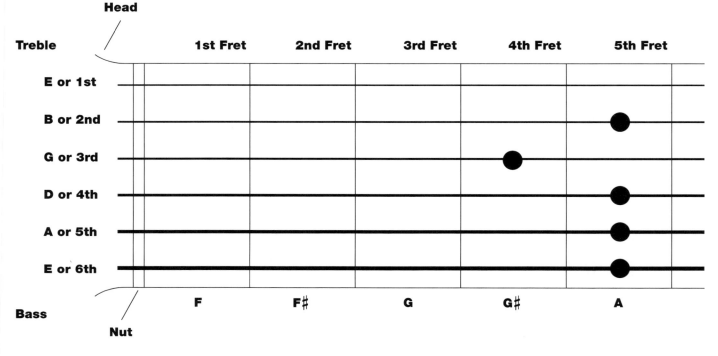

 Press down where indicated, one at a time, following the instructions below.

Estimate the pitch of the 6th string as near as possible to **E** or at least a comfortable pitch (not too high or you might break other strings in tuning up).

Then, while checking the various positions on the above diagram, place a finger from your left hand on:

The 5th fret of the E or 6th string and **tune the open A** (or 5th string) to the note (A)

The 5th fret of the A or 5th string and **tune the open D** (or 4th string) to the note (D)

The 5th fret of the D or 4th string and **tune the open G** (or 3rd string) to the note (G)

The 4th fret of the G or 3rd string and **tune the open B** (or 2nd string) to the note (B)

The 5th fret of the B or 2nd string and **tune the open E** (or 1st string) to the note (E)

Chord Boxes

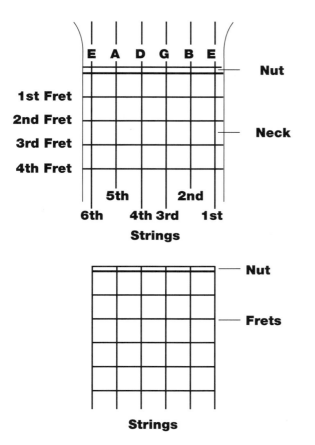

E A D G B E

Nut

1st Fret
2nd Fret
Neck
3rd Fret
4th Fret

5th   2nd
6th   4th 3rd   1st
Strings

Nut

Frets

Strings

The A Chord

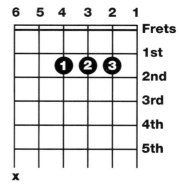

6 5 4 3 2 1

Frets
1st
① ② ③
2nd
3rd
4th
5th

x

x = do not play this string

All chords are major chords unless otherwise indicated.

Chord boxes are diagrams of the guitar neck viewed head upwards, face on, as illustrated in the above drawings. The horizontal double line at the top is the nut, the other horizontal lines are the frets. The vertical lines are the strings starting from E or 6th on the left to E or 1st on the right.

Any dots with numbers inside them simply indicate which finger goes where. Any strings marked with an **x** must not be played.

The fingers of your hand are numbered 1, 2, 3, & 4 as in the diagram below.

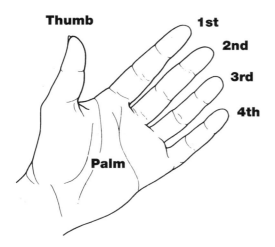

Thumb   1st
2nd
3rd
4th

Palm

Left Hand
Place all three fingers into position and press down firmly. Keep your thumb around the middle of the back of the neck and directly behind your 1st and 2nd fingers.

Right Hand Thumb Or Plectrum
Slowly play each string, starting with the 5th or A string and moving up to the 1st or E string.

If there is any buzzing, perhaps you need to:-
Position your fingers nearer the metal fret (towards you); or adjust the angle of your hand; or check that the buzz is not elsewhere on the guitar by playing the open strings in the same manner.

Finally, your nails may be too long, in which case you are pressing down at an extreme angle and therefore not firmly enough. Also the pad of one of your fingers may be in the way of the next string for the same reason.

So, cut your nails to a more comfortable length and then try to keep them as near vertical to the fretboard as possible.

Once you have a 'buzz-free' sound, play the chord a few times and then remove your fingers and repeat the exercise until your positioning is right instinctively.

Holding The Guitar

The picture above shows a comfortable position for playing rock or pop guitar

The Right Hand
When STRUMMING (brushing your fingers across the strings), hold your fingers together.

When PICKING (plucking strings individually), hold your wrist further away from the strings than for strumming.

Keep your thumb slightly to the left of your fingers which should be above the three treble strings as shown.

The Plectrum
Many modern guitar players prefer to use a plectrum to strike the strings. Plectrums come in many sizes, shapes and thicknesses and are available from your local music shop.

Start with a fairly large, soft one if possible, with a grip. The photo shows the correct way to hold your plectrum.

The Left Hand
Use your fingertips to press down on the strings in the positions described. Your thumb should be behind your 1st and 2nd fingers pressing on the middle of the back of the neck.